I0569153

THE GIRL WITH SALEM IN HER EYES

Also from Ann Marie Eleazer

She's Magic & Midnight Lace

The Girl With
SALEM
In Her Eyes

a collection of poetry & prose

ANN MARIE ELEAZER

300 SOUTH MEDIA GROUP | NEW YORK

Copyright © 2022 Ann Marie Eleazer

All rights reserved.

No part of this book may be reproduced in any form or by any electronic or mechanical means including information storage and retrieval systems, without permission in writing from the publisher or author.

The only exception is for book reviews or articles written about the book and/or authors.

This book is presented as a collection.

ISBN-13: 978-1-957596-09-9 | Paperback

First Printing September 2022
Cover Design by Indie Author Solutions
Published by 300 South Media Group

Table of Contents

Dedicated to all of the Autumn souls with a bit of witch and wickedness laced through their veins.

Haunted Novella

Forever a haunted, Gothic novella
in a world of rushed affairs
and romantic novels.
Her enchanted, ghostly chambers
are not for the faint at heart.

For Those Who Wait

For the dark beauties who wait, with tucked wings,
for the first dying tree;
the change in wind,
and the growing silence of the woods;
who come alive in bat-blackened nights,
chilly days
and swags of leaves,
sleek and golden glazed in dragon flame reds and oranges,
emerging and breathing a sigh of relief
as autumn makes her presence known
and the ghost-grey skies settle in.

Perfect Combination

Some girls were born of
forest witches,
crow wishes
and a blend of
moonlight
&
magic.

Tuck me Away

I fight these bright days
and warmer winds to come.
The ache for hibernation heady upon the tip of my tongue.
Tuck me away with sangria and sage,
with the promise of a stroll on a chilly day.
And when the sun kisses my lashes just right,
let me not forget the craving
for the deep, dark night...
fetching voices,
ethereal songs,
the aroma of treats,
his and hers appetites.

𝕸idnight Strolls

Her ghosts take up residence with the goddess in her soul,
while taking her poetry by the hand
for a midnight stroll.
They know her deepest,
darkest secrets
and remind the men
who they're dealing with.

Vintage Love Letters

She is a vintage love letter
full of dirty words and manic birds.
A blessing and a curse,
the ballad and the verse.
Lilac scented lust.
Always the October moon,
but fiery as a southern sun.

Poetic Bookworm

I'm that bookworm,
dreamy and quiet,
enchanting and solitary.
And then nightfall arrives…
he shows up in my thoughts
and I'm dark sips,
poetry,
moody
and magic dust.
*And oh how I love to be haunted
in all the right places…*

Ruffled Wings

Just ask the night cats lurking about
and the ill at ease winds that blow to and fro,
they know her ruffled wings so well
and the familiar scent, of another life,
when she was a thunderous,
daring,
sharp-tongued
Queen CROW.

Spooky One

I'll always be a spooky girl
living in my own dark little world,
with spirits and sable-colored crayons
to keep me company.

Autumn's Death

In autumn's death
and its bewitching allure of darkness
is where she's most alive.
Where her aches begin to dance
and her hunger knows no bounds.

Darkened Silk

October slipped between my nooks and crannies
like the soft nip of a spell.
A deep lull that can only
be cast upon by days
dressed in the finest of darkened silk.

That Special One

It takes a special kind of man
to handle her darkness
and play in her magic,
just as only a certain love for her would do.
The dark side; tormented,
looming and final.
The kind mystery thrillers,
with haunted backdrops
are made of.

Gothic Revival

And if the Gothic revival,
black elegant,
magically mysterious,
wander me through a castle in the middle of the night,
as the candles dance
and the wind screams outside
dress fits,
then drape yourself in it
and let your inner witch
glow.

Love Me That Way

Love me in the way your darkness
craves my shadow when she plays
hard to get,
and as the souls of our crows
mate evermore
'til death do them part.

Women Like Her

A woman like her will haunt you
happily ever after or until death knocks upon your door.
Singing spells,
wedding bells
and a pretty little casket to hell.
(Tenderly unearthly and terribly untamed)

Kindling Thoughts Me

Some days a field of wild violets
and wicked thoughts
that need kindling.
Other days an eerie trail
amongst haunted limbs
and legends that won't rest.

October Glow

She loves this time of year.
Her skin takes on an October glow
and her dark, autumn-like angels
start peeking through.
Days turn moody;
nights slip deeper into a spell
when everything is dipped in hues
of fire,
brimstone
and deep, eerie euphoria.

Autumn Moss

She wears her magic as the trees
wear gowns of flame and fog.
Rainswept thoughts,
autumn moss
and eyes that glisten in witchcraft.

Nor a Soul

There is not a soul that
shines as vivid as the one
drenched in shades of saffron,
softly and sadly falling upon
ancient graveyards,
while dancing with the wind
on an autumn afternoon.

Mischievous Monsters

She didn't scare the crows.
They adored her.
Protected her.
Kept pace with the voices in her head,
and those mischievous monsters
under her bed.
And when the sinister stories
came to play,
they perched atop her throne
and sent them all away.

October Girl

She is an October girl...
dark lace,
shades of violet,
honeyed hues
and tempestuous storm clouds.
You will find her amongst the
dead leaves,
with her collection of
chestnuts and skulls.

Witch's Soul

With a witch's soul
and a heart raised by
black & white movies,
the darker side of the season
grows within me.

Lace & Longing

Pretty little thing...
laced in the scent of
dark rain,
wild berries
& night tulips.
She longed for his darkness
and his bed of dead fronds.

A Late September Evening

She's a late September evening
at the tip of twilight…
dark wine,
that feline smirk of roguery to come,
and the air whispering its intentions
for a little sin and sorcery.

This Time of Year

I do love this time of year
when the sweet summer scents
and silky smiles of
lovers' lagoons
and lady slippers begin to say goodbye.
When the love affair between death and trees,
the ground and leaves begin.
The velvet shades of darker days
and the tingling giggles
of witches in the air.
Tis autumn tapping her magic at our door.

Awaken Me

Nothing awakens me as autumn does.
Draped in her strange perfume
and otherworldly webs.
I am, at last, home.

Her Arrival

She'll arrive by way of
magic sprig,
broomstick
or crow
depending upon her mood,
and which way the wind blows.

It's Beginning to

It's beginning to smell a lot like
witchcraft
&
screaming mums
around here.

Brown—Eyed Girl

Brown eyes...
painted in vintage sepia ruins
and amber nightfall.
Mysterious, inky and irresistible
like a beast drawn to his honey.
Autumn fairytales
and love affairs between
purple rains and forest primroses.
Pure magic.

Wings & Witchcraft

The way she wears her
wings and witchcraft…
ever so elegantly,
mysteriously.
Scarlet letters and epitaphs
engraved upon her heart
flying her towards her
deepest needs
and desires.

Hallows Eve

If Halloween were a woman she
would resemble the darkest rose;
thorns as sharp and silky as the October sky,
smelling of night tulips and mist,
with muddy lips,
amethyst hips
and petals black as pitch.
You will find her dancing with the witches
and sipping on midnight margueritas
with her ancestors
in the full moonlight.

Black Irises

Give me a man smelling of black irises
and dark mood
covered in
silky, stormy night air.
A man matching my intentions,
ready to cast spells
and create love potions together.

Moonflowers

I don't get lost in the dark.
I play there growing sprigs of
moonflowers
whilst falling hopelessly
and endlessly
in love.

Portals

I was never graceful or delicate.
I've always been carefully wrapped
in dark euphoria
and portals
to forgotten realms.

Moody Bitch

Some days I don't want to be
soft and sanguine.
I just want to be a
dark, moody bitch
and weep ink to my heart's content

Let Her Breathe

Today, I will bathe myself in rain
and let my darkness breathe.
Because what storytellers don't tell you
is that most belles are borne of
beasts,
thistles
and petals
long dead and fallen.

Conversations with the Moon

I don't want lucid and logical.
I want breathless and bewitching.
Those who talk to the moon
while dripping in charms.
Those who think they are baskets of spring violets,
but deep-down
smell like gloom-misted skin.

Granddaughters

We may be the granddaughters
of the witches they weren't able to burn,
but our souls belong to the
full moon
and the crows
that watched over them.

Dreams

I'm temptress-laced dreams,
witch-kissed weather
and nights drenched in old-fashioned thirst.
Dress me in Gothic romance
atop a Victorian staircase,
and don't wake me when it's over.

Secret Tunnels

Her sorrow is full of sorcery
and secret, wicked tunnels.
Wildly tamed
and gently feral.
A storybook you should read alone.

Where You'll Find Her

I find my soul hidden away in solitude,
breathing a sigh of relief
in the embrace of an
old forest witch...
and when I'm not looking,
she's in her best red,
taunting the wolves
and counting their pleas.

Fairy Aesthetic

I was never drawn to the comfort of
iridescent, ivory-winged angels.
I waited for the seduction of night fairies
arriving under the cover of shadow,
to put my sins
and demons to the test.

Where the Oleanders Are

Among the ominous oleanders
in Dracula's garden
and the wild black birds
that visit there,
is where you will find her.

My Tea

I'll never beg your pardon
for my howls
and hisses,
the fullness of my moons
and the hunger of my moods.
The way I take my tea…
The way I do me.

A Girl's Best Friend

They say diamonds are a girl's best friend,
but mine were always
dark forces
that caught me by surprise,
and sent me reeling
into poetic, passionate places.

Falling in Love

Crows are women
who fell in love with their darkness
and never came back.
If the darkened wind took me,
I wouldn't return either…

Where the Wicked Roam

I tend to roam where the
black butterflies loom
and upon the tendrils of wind
roused by a witch's broom.
Under black velvet skies
and in my dark poet's embrace.
Amongst corvids,
haunted bookshops
and the remains of old lace.

Claims & Flames

He's the dark wisps to my soft sips;
the temptation to my intrigue.
He reached in and claimed my garden jasmine
and turned it into flaming leaves.

Foliage

Her blood type is various shades of foliage,
with a hint of forest flair
dancing upon her skin.
And when he comes knocking
upon her haunted cottage,
she'll be sure to let him in.

Dark Explosions

I'll forever have that autumn blush,
with black roses painted
on the walls of my soul,
but the way he comes at me
with darkened delight,
makes the heat of summer explode in me
like the hottest July night.

Street Fairs

Even on warm days
my mind wanders through unholy paths
dreaming of Salem street fairs,
the awakening of lady ghosts
in dark floral gowns,
and curling up by fairy lights
to the sounds of sinister weather
outside the window.

Ambrosia

As others welcomed
the soft caress of spring,
she filled her nest with fresh feathers,
a few full moons
and jars of ambrosia
awaiting the deep touch of autumn
once again.

Special Blend

Be careful how you sip, my dear.
Her special blend of
sorcery,
sensuality
and
splendor
have been known to turn
even the most suspecting men
into skittish deer.

Secret Ingredient

The secret ingredients were always
you,
me
and the autumn moon
with stray cats
and strange magic
flowing through our veins.

All That She Is

She's savory and strange.
Brown sugar and black tea.
Harvest moons and horror movies.
And the sweet smell of dead trees.

Unearthly

I'm always ready for misty, moody mornings;
cloudy, quiet afternoons
and magical nights, by candlelight
with Sally and Gillian.
That unearthly,
soothing feeling
only they can bring.

Confessions

Love letters
Secret diaries
Folded notes in hidden places
Her handwritten confessions to the ghosts…
it's all **poetry**, darling.

Come Have a Taste

She has that vintage tasting,
bed of black roses,
witch-like,
vixen-eyed heart.

Life Goals

I want to be the mysterious lady
who lives in a cottage
deep in the forest,
with my flower pots,
hanging glass chimes
and black gowns strung on the line.
I want a Gomez-type lover
and a murder of crows for pets.
The children are afraid to visit on Halloween
so, we leave bowls of candy and trinkets
near the entrance gate
with pumpkins and lights all aglow.
These are some of my life goals.

Take Me To

~Dark Caves
~Abandoned Castles
~Secret Forests
~Secluded Cottages
~Antique Shops
~Old Cemeteries
~Vintage Bookshops
~Haunted Seaside Towns

Give me a pair of worn, antique shoes
that have spun a dance or two;
a stained-glass window in a forgotten farmhouse;
empty perfume bottles imprinted with a lover's fingertips;
forbidden love letters tucked away
in a dusty attic;
a vintage soul who yearns to dance with mine.

Magical Ones

Those magical ones;
all thunder and roaring veins;
witchcraft and wild lilacs,
who have been long captured by the
worn pages of a book.
The ones who find stars in cloudy skies,
and love in lost quotes,
while their hearts tremble in the arms
of dark, old-fashioned love songs.

Weekends

Adorning myself in the war paint of my witch spirit,
the shadowy
primal prose
of my poet
and lovely things
that often grown in
strange,
dark places.
Some of my favorite weekend pastimes.

Ancestral Backbones

Some pray;
others scream promises in the dark
and recite poetry to their ghosts.
And while the witch of our past,
imbedded deeply within looks on,
some do all three...

Stoker Love

And then there are those of us
who turn Saturday night fairytales
into Sunday morning poetry.
Warm spooning,
ravenous appetites,
lampshades covered in discarded silk
and the greedy need
to pick up where we left off
in the middle of our Bram Stoker love story.

Season of the Witch

Tis the season
when prowling cats
famished ghosts,
temptress-laced dreams
and mad, magical girls
come out to play.

Fix Those Pointy Hats

Crowns are overrated.
Give me the ones who will straighten
my pointy hat;
match my magic
and stir up my positive powers.
The ones whose broomsticks
are at the ready when it all goes down.
Those are my kind of witchy bitches.

Much Love

Much love to the
dark, folk-tale witches
my eyes so longingly gazed at as a little girl,
who showed me what life can be like
when we decide we don't want
to be the princess
at the end of the story.

Under the Bed

Sometimes the lady in his bed…
and sometimes the monster under it.
And, oh, how he loves it.
More often than not looking over my shoulder
when I come with one voice put away
and the other ready to play.

Misunderstood

Magical creatures are often misunderstood
with their tousled hair
and wicked affairs of the air.
They are what dreams of
dried, dead things
are made of.

Beautifully Bleak

While the steam of summer
surrounds me,
I shall pretend
I am on the balcony
of my mysterious mansion
clothed in 1800s linen,
where the sky
is beautifully chilly
& bleak.

Unswept

And as the primroses were afraid
to get wet
and unswept,
she danced in thunderstorms,
drinking the rain
and making potions
in mud puddles.

Conversing With Blackbirds

Some prefer to
bathe on the beach
or play in the city.
But my heart ached to get lost in
haunted villages;
wandering old graveyards,
conversing with blackbirds
and ancient tale tellers
full of sordid,
scented secrets.

Saving Myself

I don't care what the damsels would do
or who is over the rainbow.
I want to fly amongst lightening
and violet clouds,
upon feathers
and boughs
with a pocket full of wisdom
and a Queen's desire,
protecting what's mine
and saving myself.

Trick or Treat

He came ready to deceive
with his box of tricks,
only to discover her bag of treats
already devised to devour him.
You can't go playing trick~or~treat
on a woman with
magic lips
and dancing,
poetic finger tips.

All Hallows Eve

All Hallows Eve stirs
feline cries within me;
soaks my senses in glorious hocus pocus
and makes my skin dance
to the color of red,
untouched lips
and the vibe of poets
long gone.

Let Me Out

It's a perfect Autumn day
to let my dark, pretty heart out
to pulse and play.
The kind of day where the dark wildflower in me
says I must go.

A Mother's Young

Don't ever mess with a mother's young,
for she has the power of a **witch**;
the bite of **wolf**,
and the claws of a **cat**
to silently
and, with a smirk upon her face,
ambush you.

Soul Collector

While other little girls collected
dolls,
trinkets
and toys,
she was busy gathering
ghost stories,
spider silk
and pretty little jars of venom
for misbehaved boys.

Courtyard of Bones

Lost is where I long to be
atop a darkened throne
in my cottage courtyard of bones
wearing nothing but solitude
and midnight lace.

Demise & Daisies

I'm an antiquated implication,
night-hearted
and opaque-minded.
A whirlwind of demise
and daisies.
You'll never figure me out
and that's okay.
You're not meant to.

Skull Whisperer
She's...

a witch's caress;
that soothing flavor of chilly,
windy nights
and
the skull whisperer.
A forever Autumn in Salem kind of girl.

Greedy Wolves

My melancholy
and magic
dance to the same tune.
Both seeped deeply within me,
shifting untamed thoughts into love spells
and polished stones into greedy wolves.

A Soft Grasp

I long for a time that no longer exists,
a place I once belonged.
The ancient,
magical secrets
whisper to me
when its deathly quiet
and her soft fingers
gently grasp me by my throat.

Feeding Time

Excuse me while I get lost
in my potions
and poetry.
The world has been harsh lately
and my soul needs to feed.

Woman Cave

Deep in my woman cave
where my damsel rests
and my dragon rekindles
her magic cinders.
Where there is silence,
19th century lovers
and a rainy, Sunday-like
soul squeeze that feeds my wild rose.

Her Magic

Sometimes,
all a woman has left to hold onto
is her magic
and sometimes,
her magic is the secret ingredient
to all that awaits her.
*(There is nothing more powerful
than when a woman's poetry
and the spells of her inner witch collide)*

Cursed

Forever cursed with an
amorous heart and a fairy-like wonder
who falls for foxes
and feral lovers,
dripping promises
and pet names
dancing from their lips.

Cravings

She craved wondrous,
wicked things.
The sort of beautiful things that left her
dizzy
and daydreaming…
prone to getting into trouble.
The best kind of trouble with
mischief
and moon dust involved.

No Escape

I followed my soul
down the rabbit hole where I
knew I was meant to be.
She grasped my hand,
the magic began
and we got drunk
on adventure and tea.

Where Teal Things Roam
She's...

Skull bones & silk petals;
teal gowns & thunder clouds;
a witch's poem
&
where the bush clovers roam.

Unbothered

She's of wild animals
and Wonderland frolics…
dark angels,
things that prowl
impulses that sing.
You'll find her unbothered amongst her
fox glove crowns,
vintage gowns
and pretty things.

In the Cobwebs

I'll never be a
blow away the cobwebs kind of girl.
I need to rest there with murmurs
from sweet mouths cloaked
in sheer madness.

Dark Edge of Things

It's your darkness
that will tell you
who
what
when
and where...
and how to get there.
(forever the soul skulking on the dark edge of things)

Magic Wands

Be careful how you play her magic wand.
It may be frayed and moth-eaten,
but there's an enchanted sword under there,
and it doesn't give second chances.

Beauty Marks

I loved the way he knew how to read my incantations…
the dark ones.
The ones invited through my garden gates not many others
were allowed to go.
Places that awaken me in faraway lands,
wearing nothing but a pretty hat
and his favorite scent.
The ones that find me in the middle of a
feast fit for a beast
and beauty marks covering my thighs.
The ones where the wolves fall at my feet
and stocking-clad witches take notes.

Leather & Lace

The Stevie Nicks songs in my soul
can't take their eyes off
the sorcery in yours.
Let's make a little magic,
and a little thunder,
while our leather and lace fall in love.

Black

Whether her gowns
or crowns,
she wears them **black**
with a touch of
hidden passion
&
madness.

Potions & Possession

From the moment we began writing
each other's darkest fantasies,
his words captured me
mind,
body
and soul.
Our scriptures laced with
possession
and passion;
our potions spiked with
taboo
and temptation.
His melodies made love to me
before his mouth ever did.

Day & Night

She's fields of wildflowers by day...
a dark forest by night.
The thorn of the rose,
the dirty love notes
to the pretty prose.
Feral,
fairylike,
foreboding.

Be You

Women should be anything & all they want to be…
~Gothic Sorceress
~Wolf Temptress
~Full Moon Goddess
~Enchanted Witch
~Mysterious Fairy
~Solitary Siren
~Bold Bitch
~Mama Bear
~Whatever makes her happy~

Ber Months

Summer breezes
bring lurid teases
& luscious eternal rest
as the 'ber months descend
upon us.

Rousing

He rouses magic from so deep within me,
(my witch, my raven and my cupboard brimful of secret ingredients)
even my demons won't attempt
to venture there.
A love meant only for him and I,
under twilight skies,
where our creatures playfully
and hungrily reside.

Roses & Coal

You will find her
between the pages of
strange fiction,
a dark poetry soul,
with a heart of
manic roses
and stockings
full of coal.

Oh Sylvia

She writes things she would never say aloud…
those which torment her,
arouse her,
and make her mad like an
out of tune melodeon
trapped in Sylvia's head.
*(She made madness look magical
and a Sylvia poem
the loveliest of the devil's interval)*

Truth or Dare

Be careful when you do her wrong.
Her darkness will haunt you.
Her damsels will write about you.
And her unforgiving aura will
drag you to hell for a game of
truth or dare.

Where I'll Be

If you want to come play with me,
I'll be swinging between the autumn clouds
and the deepest, darkest corners
of your mind.

Ancient Queen

Ancient Queen,
full of glint and moonlight;
hidden caves,
vintage vines
and haunted trees.
She arrives like blustery-brushed
witch weather
and leaves with
a scent of intention.
Even the ghosts
watch from a distance.

Smooth As the Moon

She's one of those mad girls,
full of magic
and sad symphonies,
jagged tea cups
and smooth whiskey.
If you look closely at the night sky,
you'll see her pulsating back and forth
between the moon
and hell.

Foreboding

Her heart is a foreboding, frosty little thing…
deep and velvety,
wrapped delicately in
longing and lady gloves.
Be careful not to scare it.
I heard it bites
and never lets go.

For the Imaginative Ones

For the ones who grew up
in Matilda's solitude,
Coraline's hidden tunnels
and in backyards making brews
with mud and sticks;
whose imaginary friends
flew them on wings to forest creeks
and abandoned castles on cliffs
to dine with queens.
And whose imaginations
inscribed every adventure,
in secret diaries,
so that one day,
she could present the world
her poetic soul.

Wishing Wells

Little girls who throw pennies
into wishing wells,
grow up to be women
who cast magic spells,
and make them come true.

That Dark Love

The darker the love,
the deeper the magic.
Under her dark wings
he finds himself tucked and tended to,
coated in her emerald-colored secrets of Eden
and ravenous chambers.

Hiding Sprees

Away from reality
has always been my favorite place to be.
Traipsing through fog
or on a hiding spree.
Amongst my otherworldly desires,
wrapped in beautifully dark skies.
Tucked into hidden crevices
and out of the way of prying eyes.

Autumn Girls

Autumn girls are forest girls;
jade goddesses turned
flaming seers;
moods bathed in melody
and misery.
Strange, magical creatures
with ancient hearts,
and minds full of
pastures that have fallen into
a deep slumber.

Across Town

Meanwhile, across town,
I could feel his darkness
and taste his magic...
tousled
and tangled need.
My poison garden bloomed along my skin
as the scent of his thoughts
beckoned me to his side of the forest,
watching with impatience
as he readied the bed
and sharpened his claws.

Enamored

Forever enamored with haunted blessings
and bizarre minds;
lingering daydreams,
the color of hopeless romantics
and the way his wicked words
tease me throughout the day.

Autumnal

She's the one who escapes to
tender arms
cradled in beautiful chaos
and wakes up pulling
raven feathers from her hair.
The perfect blend of a
fairy in a floral gown,
a harlot in a hooded cape.

Let's Sing and Dance

Her poetry loves to sing
and slow dance,
but on nights like tonight,
all it wants to do is bare its teeth
and take a bite.

Treasure Trove

She bleeds words with a twinge of
sad, brilliant magic.
War and midnight blue violets
long left through the cracks of a haunted house.
A treasure trove of
teardrops, chaos
and messy, mysterious ways.
Alluring and enchanting as a starlit night
and a moon that shares her secrets back.

Grudges

I'm a darkly creature,
with tendrils of spiraling serpents
and a singed spine
of wisteria vines
where crows
and grudges seek shelter.

Lineal Queens

Many a man have tried to eat my heart,
but you can't hurt a woman with the
burning embers
of lineal queens howling
through her seams,
and the protection of the full moons
they called upon.

All That She Is

She's a mingle of magical places
and orchards where poison apples grow.
And while some dream of bluebirds
over the rainbow,
she craves the smell of autumn
where wild, inviting eyes make their home.

She Goes

And when the forest calls,
she goes,
for she is
magic dust
and poetic lust,
with an appetite writhing in
things that
love in the dark.

Her Perfume

Inviting she was like the hint of October's perfume
on a windy summer's day...
or the sea witch's promise of true love
in a wicked, tempting sort of way.

Seamstress

Those hauntingly floral spells,
decorated ever so delicately in spikes,
the catch of unsuspecting breaths
and the tulle of a foregone seamstress...
an autumn dream you didn't see coming
and one you may not want to awaken from.

Dead Flowers & Fangs

She'll enrapture you with
pretty words and poetic potions,
while her ghosts decide if they
want to slow dance with you once upon a fairytale
or love you straight to hell in her
handbag full of
dead flowers
and fangs.

She Is the Rain

She's slivers of daffodils and demons…
the witchery of rainy days
and, some days,
she is the rain.

Eat You Alive

Beware her fragrant, dark florals.
The scent of her delicate petals
and her lilting tongue
will have you falling in love
while her thorns,
all cat-like, downy
and full of sweet desperation
slowly bury you alive.

Dark Circus

There are moments her head is a dark circus,
a land of miscast spells.
It runs off to play with creepy calla lilies
like men in cheap hotels.

Shhh

I could tell you a story about a queen,
but they come far and few between.
For powerful goddesses,
witches,
magic mothers
&
lady lovers
are far too often feared
and left unseen.

Raven Thoughts

She was all raven thoughts
and locks of sooty silk;
dark violet moods and buried treasure…
oh, her buried treasure,
the kind dirty romance novels
and thrift store storybooks
are made of.

All of Us

There are many women inside me...
**wicked, weepy
sensual, shaded
tragic, magical**
& then there's my **ghost.**

Private Party

I desire my magic potions laced with
virtue and venom
a delicious blend of slow dances
and wrist-fastened walls.
Where orchids and ivy run wild…
lust-scented skirts,
gentle lovers
and a private party for two.

Not Available

She's not available today.
Her nostalgia has summoned her
and asked her out to play.
For she is the Elphaba side of spring
in a chasing lily pads,
lick of thunder on her skin,
dark simper of pollinating gardens
sort of way.

Wicked Poetess

Wicked poetess,
full of absinthe and red wine.
Enchantments interlace her fingertips
and crawl sensually up her spine.
Bringing ink to life
and words many daydream about,
but dare not say.

Love Her All or Love Her Not She's...

Elegance and evil;
pin-up and poetry;
sapphires and skulls;
velvety and volcanic;
moonlight and madness.
Love her all or love her not.

Love Potion

~Lock of lover's hair
~Black rose petals
~Dark chocolate
~Whisk of enchantment
~Dash of seduction
Serve in a skull goblet

Our love,
dark and divine
sloe-eyed and silky
will forever stand
the test of ancient time.

Dark Ode

She's a dark ode
to the poetic spells that
spill from mouths
swaddled in
flames and frost.
The ones whose pockets full of posies
burst in purrs
and screams.
Whose solace mingles with restless spirits
and wanders through haunted groves.
Their desires always end up covered in mud and twigs.

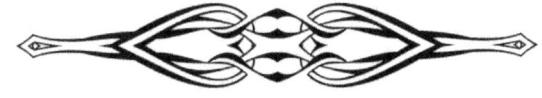

Things I Would Tell My Younger Self

~Dark fairytales do come true
~Your swords are sharper than pretty words spilling from the lips of
hungry wolves
~Fairy godmothers are real
~It's okay to prefer moonbathing to sunbathing
~You're a goddess and have the ashes of witches dancing in your veins
~Gardens also need darkness to bloom

Gothic Romance

My shyness is but seedlings of
black beauty pansies aching to bloom;
my boldness, tangled in wilding weeds,
seeks fine dining with voracious appetites
and a haunted side of
classic Gothic romance.

Death—like

Those foreboding castle stairways
bring me back to a time when
witches and queens,
dark and wicked in nature,
roamed the lands and the books in my hands.
And I,
but with a
wild-eyed, curious heart
begged to be swept up
into the wings
of their disquieting-like counterparts.

Morbid Twist

Whether magic mirrors,
wardrobes
or brick roads,
my breath forever sighs
for bewitching plots
with a morbid twist…
darkened paws,
stinging cyclones,
that poison bliss.

The Quiet Ones

Don't let the quiet whispers
in her eyes mislead you.
She breathes fire
and puts magic spells
on unsuspecting hearts.
Dark ruby eyes
and
black glitter thighs.

Happily Autumn After

I'll happily ever after
be lost in rainy, Autumn days.
Haunted picnics in the hollow
and fistfuls of heartbeats
under cloudy skies.
Professing our love
in the deep end of an abandoned cemetery forest
as our spirit mates look on.

The Plath to His Poe

The Plath to his Poe.
The cordial sadness
to his reclusive soul…
my wild feline wrestles
with the soft seduction
simmering behind my tongue
and I wonder how I shall
take him on this rainy, dead-like day.

Erotic Tales

She's spun of erotic tales
and blurred boundaries;
soft poetry with a
come hither look
and claws that cling for days.
(Brown eyes full of sorcery and soft, silent screams)

Eager Creatures

Not flowers, nor fanciness can capture me
as much as your fondness for blanket forts and The Birds.
I want to play with the creatures
that stir within your soul;
eager
enamored
bothered
and
bewitched.

Lush Melancholy

Darkness wraps me in her
lush melancholy this time of year…
shadow, thunderstorms,
the edge of the forest begging to be known
in that sinister, sultry way.
And on nights the heat of summer changes
into her best black dress,
he and I will be all
teeth and tongue
hums and howls.

War Cries

Evanora's war cry
soft sage tones
and sips
of Spanish fly.
You can either get out of her way
or stand by her side.

Autumn Souls

So uniquely different
and darkly vibrant.
Opaque shores
and low beating hearts.
That haunting, "I'm not alone" feeling
when the clouds,
tinged with a hint of demise in the air,
roll in.
She'll unwrap her insanity and hold it a little bit closer
as the hint of dew upon her locket
brings Fall to life.

Singing Sorcery

You can take her out of the
folk tale and the forest,
dress her up and distract her with control,
but beauties who are told to keep quiet
never stray far from the singing sorcery
screaming in their souls.

Haunted Hummingbirds

Break me open
and I will drip darkness,
amongst tumbling magical secrets
and haunted hummingbirds;
antique keys to my quiet fortress
and madness…
lots and lots of
moody,
misunderstood,
melodic
madness.

Tendrils

I didn't know if it was him
or his ghosts caressing
my darkness,
but the way my back arched
and the tendrils of my desire summoned his
told me I had found home.
Maybe haunted, but still home.

You Can Be

Flower and the fire.
Wear the crown and the crow's feathers.
Soft and savage.
Sensual and standoffish.
Carry the sword
while wearing the silk dress.
Effervesce and ash.

𝕸𝖞 𝕯𝖆𝖗𝖑𝖎𝖓𝖌

To be Wendy Darling in Autumn
looking for stars and euphoria
in chilled, flightless skies.
I'm slipping into a scarlet slumber
while sipping philters
from his lips
and wondering if I belong in Neverland
or if there's no place like home.

Vintage Maiden

I think I awoke in the wrong time.
Lay me on a bed of rain clouds
and let me go back.
After all,
I'm forever forged in
witchcraft and **Wonderland**.

Deathly Murmurs

I'll forever adore my
ruby red petals and the way they
dance under radiant beams,
but ever more shall I cherish
the withered and pallid murmur
of my decaying leaves,
as the winds begin to rustle
and the witches,
watching on the horizon,
wave me home.

Dark Summer

Give me that savory taste of the
dark side of summer
steeped in stormy nights
and fireflies at twilight.
Sultry sighs,
purple skies
and black butterflies.
Sensual moons
and the air's moody, mysterious caress.
Hidden kisses bathed
in secrets and spells
and forests that never go to sleep.

Blooming

She blooms in baby's breath,
flushed of fever and forevermore,
but loves in hues of deadly nightshade.
Full of hysteria,
hunger
and screeching graveyards.

Summer Dream Vacation

~Salem
~Exploring Witch Museums
~Strolling haunted cemeteries
~Wandering magic markets
~A visit with the Sanderson sisters
~Indulging in ancient feasts & rituals
~Stocking up on broomsticks, oils & magical elixirs

I Am Her

My darkness comes only in sanguine
and sacrosanct flavors.
Don't try to mend her,
taunt her,
or persuade her with
bouquets of solace.
She rides with winter lungs,
upon frigid wings
and tends to the
deepest parts of me.
She is me.
I am her.
And we are one.

Beware

Beware the ones whose souls
are made of Autumn
for they are magic...
wild, wicked, glorious magic.
(Matildas who grow up to be Maleficents)

Her Tea Party

(By invitation only)
Strange creatures
Loyal bitches
Secret keepers
Brooding lovers
Enchanters
Spiked tea
Passion potion
Velvet cakes
Madness welcomed

Once Upon a Misty Time

There was a woman who loved
misty mornings
filled with brews,
magic
and the company of crows.
And even darker nights
spilled with yearnings,
lost minds
and the chanting
of her predatory adventures.

Inner Magic

As she gets lost,
her inner magic comes alive.
Her feathers unfurl
and the chaotic intricacies woven
into her words
scatter like soothing lyrics
and devilish ways.

Persephone

Take me to a time
where the maiden's eyes match midnight,
her dress is a bit clingy,
and her moods are restless as rainstorms.
And her men…
some gentle, and some not so much,
bashfully and boldly
guard her Persephone tendencies.

Arms of Melancholy

Ever enamored with things
forbidden and forlorn,
I often find myself wrapped in the
arms of melancholy,
never quite sure if that's where I long to be
or if love's sense of humor
is once again
playing tricks on me.

Soft Stings

She slithers and sings
upon black butterfly wings.
Sometimes a lullaby,
sometimes a sting.

Mistress

I'm more mistress of the masquerade ball
than delicate porcelain doll.
Lailah's stare
and Lilith's glare.
A sanctuary within
the eye of the storm.
Your soft Autumn kiss
and the serpent's insatiable hiss.

Seductive Curse

I'd rather be taken by
the beast's curse
than the prince's silver-plated dessert.
Ever the queen who wears her crown
and rides like the wicked witch.
The dark blossom who needs
rain and candlelight;
and rumbles of thunder to bloom.

An Ode to Practical Magic

I need that "practical magic,
living in a romantic, Victorian mansion
by the sea with my lover
and garden room" kind of life.

Cautious

Her secret garden
and silent thoughts
are as painful as Annabel Lee,
by the dark, cold sea.
Both need tending.
Both cautious who they let in.

Magic Queens

Ladies with frayed seams
and amber-colored Autumn dreams.
The ones who grew up holding hands
with their enchantments
and darkened imaginations
while places like
Sleepy Hollow
screamed in their veins.

Hanora & Assunta

I'm the one who dreams in black
and loves in pale sheets.
Always with one foot tapping gently and impatiently
in another world;
a world where my shadow twirls freely
and the lilt of my great-grandmothers' voices
sing me down the lane to where
I was meant to be.

Lace Roses

Not your average lady next door.
She's the one wandering through
gardens of gravestones,
dressed in lace roses
and lost thoughts.

Impishly Imperfect

Impish
Imperfect,
and ever so in love
with things that
join me for
midnight poetry parties
and parts of the forest
we were warned never to go.

Feast & Famine

He roused that spot in her spell book
where magic feasted
and her desires ached in famine…
dirty danced with her love-starved musings
and slow-kissed the keys
to her fortress.
That perfect bite to her soul.
The madness to her deeply,
darkly secrets he stole.

Pulsing Want

My heart dwells between the spaces of
Medusa's cold sheets
and Ophelia's velvet beats.
An otherworldly moonflower that conceals herself by day
and dances with wickedly dark skies at night.
Ancient archways to needful things
and soft, pulsing want.

Til Death

Til death does
Lucifer in you
part with Lilith in me.
Two dark hearts on a path of eternity.
Full moons,
seeping sensuality,
a love story meant to be.

The Way I Like It

I like it dark and dirty…
the love,
the skies,
the chocolate,
the hush-hush
that nobody else knows about.

Silk Cemeteries

Lips as soft as silk and fog
to disguise the Romanesque cemeteries in her eyes.
She's a small-town girl
living in her haunted realms
where beautifully tragic things
come to life.

Tousle Me

I love ruffling feathers.
Especially the
black, bewitching,
like to ruffle back kind.

Darkly Strange

I'm more low growl thoughts
and strolls through rainy-day cemeteries,
dark poetry
and deep aches
that fall from cold hearts
and burning eyes.

Black—Winged

There's a bit of black-winged fairy
in me that longs
for a romantic love affair
in a darkened wood,
and just as much a
smidgen of fireflies
glowing by way of
deathly, demanding desires
that love to come out and play.
May he bring both his
filthy and forgiving ways.

Sonatas

Not to be confused with
a 70s love song.
Beware her dark, romantic sonata.
It will pump your heartstrings
full of unrelenting thirst
while making your swooning butterflies
go mad (as a hatter).
Best of luck in your recovery…

Wrought Iron Flowers

Half of me is the garden cottage
surrounded by poison flowers;
the other half a gothic cathedral
encased in wrought iron gates.
I'm the dark words my poems whisper to you
in the middle of the night.

Dearest Ones

Debauchery disguised as darling breaths
Mary Shelley's poems and Morticia's dress.
Black ribbon upon my throat
October stars and haunted moats...
(a few of my favorite things)

A Lover's Tear

One day they will read stories about
how she rode her broom upon storm clouds
in her thorn-covered crown
and black lace dresses,
with a hint of her lover's tears
upon her lips.

Black Widow

I'm as much black widow
as I am the beast's belle.
Love laced in thorns.
My poisons
&
pleasures
travel in pairs.

Where I Belong

If you find me abandoned,
leave me be.
I belong to beautifully ancient things…
ruins,
old houses,
vintage books
& midnight flings.

Forbidden Essence

She's no place for fairytales.
You'll find her atop the prickly swirls
of the rose
and at the forbidden essence
of the apple.
Within her velvet chambers
awaiting dark touches
and teeth at the nape of her neck.

Best Red Dress

Autumn comes dressed
in her best red dress
escorted by
cashmere painted claws
and fangs
beautifully masked
in foliage and fishnet.

Feverish

The other three seasons
(even in their sometimes darkened glory)
may come and go,
But I will always be feverish
and full of twitchy appetite
For **October**.

Never Judge

Never judge a lady by her cover.
Some of us are but held together by
torn silk,
dark breaths,
broomcorn
&
the aura of improper thoughts.

That First Sip

She's that first
strong, hint of sweet,
sip of **dark poetry**
on a day where you can hear
the spirits singing,
the witches crooning
and the wind whispering spooky lullabies.

Strangled Plummeting Cries

I used to think I needed a quiet love;
one with an unruffled pulse.
But there is nothing more
beautifully disturbing than a spirit
drenched in autumn darkness,
crashing waves
and strangled, plummeting cries…
that which comes alive
in the otherworldly witching hour of night.

One Day

One day, they'll name a Gothic castle after her.
A castle fit for the ones where midnight purrs deep inside.
She'll always be more of a ghost story
than a love story kind of woman.

Velvet Clovers

Beware the mysterious ones.
The silent, but deadly types.
Those with a perfect blend of
velvet clovers,
old Hollywood secrets
&
black ice.

Where the Black Orchids Roam

You'll find her daydreaming
and night fantasizing
with a head full of
black orchids
and a heart of
impatient thoughts.

Giggles & Lace

I am at times here,
but then my little black heart becomes ill at ease
and my dark fairy comes out…
all verdigris giggles
and laced-up boots.

Witch's Ball

Sometimes I love to snuggle under the soft glow
of twinkle and his devilish delight
as we partake in dark romance and Halloween fright.
And other times I adore dressing
in my best veil and silken shawl
as he leads me by his arm to the witch's ball.

Descendants

Maybe we're the descendants of
Anne Rice,
or brides of monsters;
temptation-laced maidens
and the New England queens
who came before us.
Old souls of mad women,
whose heart songs are forever
drenched in
stifled tunes and strength
and echoes off abandoned,
bloodied walls.

Myself

October wraps me in her
strange, loving embrace
and I'm never more myself.
A dark novel & tales of magic
Sally's rag doll & Jack's meant to be
thunderstorms & crescent moons
gently haunted & wildly possessed
the grin of the pumpkin & the howl of the wind
crow's oil & sprigs of lavender
the poetess & the Autumn poem.

Burial Gowns

It's the dead hearts
that carry the most
silken
& savage of love.
Carrying burial gowns
& paper daisies
around in their pockets.

Those Midnight Ones

Heed the ones whose thoughts take over
in the middle of the night…
a black swan surrender.
They're not afraid of the dark
and will rouse yours
from its deep, death-like sleep.

Silent Screams

You'll find me in dark corners
where forbidden loves dances
and the silent screams of
Aries & Aphrodite
can be heard.

Affectionately Aloof

She wears witchcraft
as the haunted wears the woods.
As All Hallows Eve stirs her nocturnal moods
and as their shadows move together
in an aloof,
affectionate sort of way.

Mussed Up

She'd much rather be in the woods
with her hair entwined in
vines and forbidden branches.
A place where her private spaces
and unwritten pages
can be hauntingly free at last.

Softly Haunted

Roses are red,
but wild black roses are what she's made of…
softly haunted with a touch of sass.
Cold as snow with a
warm hellish glow.
Inviting, ill-mannered,
a maddening sort of misunderstanding…
a little smooth
and dark around the edges.

Her Tomb

The rain
and the ravens
know my secrets
and the sensual boneyard
blooming in my blackened tomb.

The Witch in Me

They always say they can
handle my screams...
the wild, the weepy, the witch
that makes me.
They want to hold on,
but never want to see
why my eyes turn dark
and my walls have keys.
*(I'll never apologize for at times
being a* **gloomy** *girl)*

Mud & Midnight

Her soul is but a resting place
for black birds and haunted things.
Things held tightly together
by muddied secrets and melancholy feathers.
Things she doesn't talk about,
but ever so gently sings to sleep at night
in anticipation of another day.

Deep Ends

She may be softly enchanted
on the outside,
but there will forever be a
murder of broken-hearted love birds scratching at
the back of her throat,
while wailing witches
swim relentlessly in the deep end
of her heart.

Stumbling

Ink maidens…
high off insomnia,
stumbling stars
Plath poetry
&
forbidden tea parties

Pretty Poppies

All lady and lovely when she needs to be,
but appearances can be deceiving…
she's deeply darkly and poisonous,
a witch's cloaked poppy
come evening.

Pandora

My antique tea cup is but half full of
Pandora's curses
and nestling madness;
weeping willows
and wild roses.
My bones settled above the cold tug of November
while my heart tugs for
seeping, sobbing things left behind.

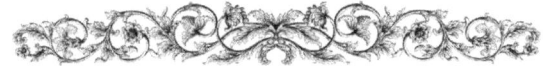

About the Author

Ann Marie Eleazer has always considered herself a bit ancient, haunted and otherworldly, who enjoys enchanted flights through the dark fairy tales and magical places she's been drawn to since childhood. What began as a creative outlet, soon became an unleashing of what lies beneath into her world of bewitching darkness and poetic passion. She began sharing her work in 2017, where she accumulated a widespread fan base and her desire to publish her work grew. A lover of all things that beautifully grow in the dark, she enjoys reading, collecting antiques, all things paranormal and filling pages with magic while spending time at her home, in the woods, with her family and furbabies.

Discover more from Author Ann Marie Eleazer at:

Facebook: facebook.com/shesmagicandmidnightlace
Instagram: instagram.com/shesmagicandmidnightlace_
Pinterest: pinterest.com/aeleazer2317
Twitter: twitter.com/she_midnight

Ann Marie's debut collection, **She's Magic & Midnight Lace**, also from 300 South Media Group, is available worldwide wherever online books are sold.

www.ingramcontent.com/pod-product-compliance
Lightning Source LLC
Chambersburg PA
CBHW051307140626
46546CB00020B/931